Tomorrow's World

LASERS IN ACTION

Lionel Bender

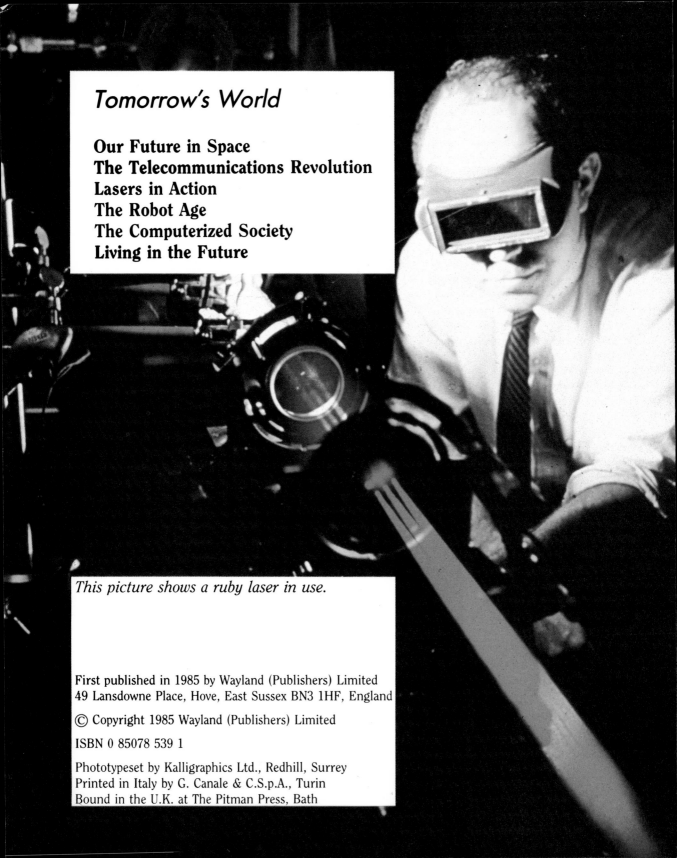

Tomorrow's World

Our Future in Space
The Telecommunications Revolution
Lasers in Action
The Robot Age
The Computerized Society
Living in the Future

This picture shows a ruby laser in use.

First published in 1985 by Wayland (Publishers) Limited
49 Lansdowne Place, Hove, East Sussex BN3 1HF, England

© Copyright 1985 Wayland (Publishers) Limited

ISBN 0 85078 539 1

Phototypeset by Kalligraphics Ltd., Redhill, Surrey
Printed in Italy by G. Canale & C.S.p.A., Turin
Bound in the U.K. at The Pitman Press, Bath

Contents

Laser light

This book will show you how lasers have changed, and will continue to change, the way we live. You have probably already seen lasers in action. The dazzling 'electronic firework' displays at pop concerts, the light shows at discos with light beams pulsing with the rhythm of the music, and the narrow beams of coloured light used as street decoration, are all the work of lasers. But there are many other uses of lasers, and some are even more dramatic.

A spectacular laser light show at a pop concert.

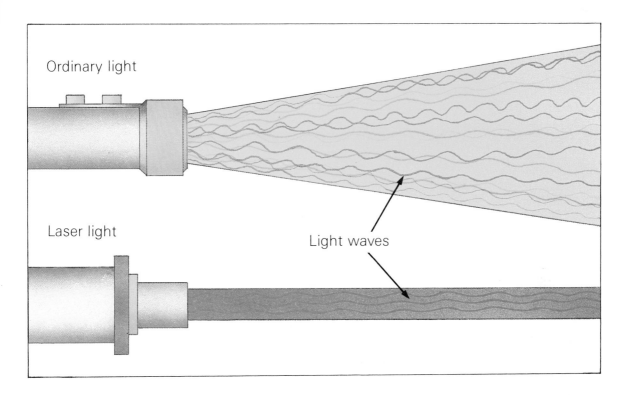

Ordinary light

Laser light

Light waves

Ordinary light is made up from waves of different colours and wavelengths, all jumbled up together. The light waves in a laser beam are all the same length and in step with each other.

What is a laser and how does it work? A laser is a device that produces a bright beam of light. The laser beam is just light, but it differs from the ordinary light of, say, a torch in three important ways. First, the light is concentrated in a narrow beam rather than spread out in all directions. The beam is straight and rod-like, and it does not fade, even over long distances. Secondly, laser light contains light of only one colour. Ordinary 'white' light, or sunlight, is a mixture of different colours. You can best see this when sunlight is split by raindrops into a rainbow – there are bands of red, orange, yellow, green, blue, indigo and violet light. These are called the spectrum.

The third difference between laser light and ordinary light concerns the light waves. All light travels in waves similar to the waves of water on the sea. The high points of the waves are known as peaks and the low points as troughs. The distance between two peaks is called the wavelength, and the number of waves a second, the frequency. In laser light, all the waves are of the same frequency and wavelength – they are identical to one another. Ordinary

5

light waves are of varying wavelength and frequency. Also, with laser light, the peaks and troughs of the waves are in step with each other in a straight line, and are said to be 'in phase'. However, with ordinary light, the waves are out of step with each other – they are jumbled up together and do not form a regular pattern. Light which is in phase is known as coherent light. Only lasers can produce such light.

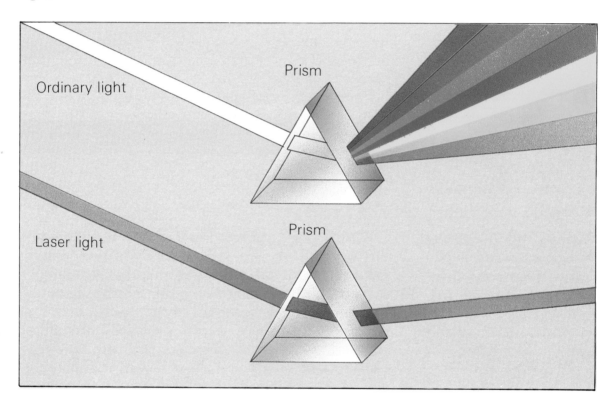

Making a laser beam

The term 'laser' comes from the first letters of the words 'Light Amplification by Stimulated Emission of Radiation'. This phrase describes how a laser beam is made. Amongst other things, lasers vary in size and power, but they all have the same four working parts: a source of energy, an active medium, an amplification system and an output unit. How these work is explained below using a ruby laser as an example. This was the first type of laser to be made, and was built by an American scientist, Dr Theodore

You can use a prism to split ordinary light into a rainbow of separate colours. Laser light, being of only one colour, does not split up when shone through a prism.

Maiman, in 1960.

A ruby laser consists of a rod of synthetic ruby crystal (the active medium), around which is coiled an electronic flash tube (the source of energy). The light energy from the lamp is absorbed by some of the atoms in the ruby rod, they then become excited, giving off their extra energy as little packets of light or 'photons'. Some photons from one excited atom hit other stimulated atoms, causing them to give off more photons. (This is the 'Stimulated Emission of Radiation' part of laser.) These photons can hit other excited atoms and produce yet more photons. The waves of light that radiate from the ruby crystal atoms therefore reinforce, or amplify, one another.

In the laser, photons spread out in all directions. Some pass through the sides of the crystal rod and are lost. To obtain maximum amplification and stimulated emission, as many photons as possible must be kept within the rod and moving along its length. This is achieved using an amplification system of two mirrors, one at each end of the ruby rod. One of the mirrors reflects back into the rod

A simplified diagram of a ruby laser.

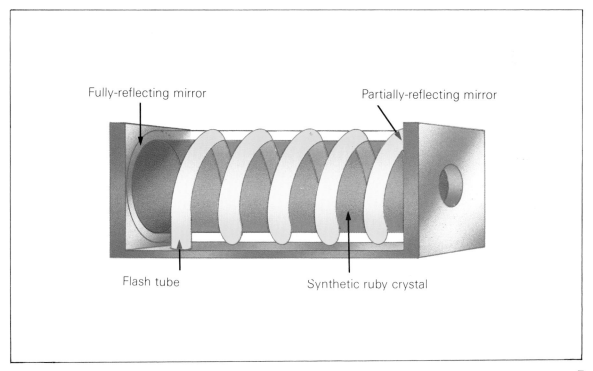

Fully-reflecting mirror

Partially-reflecting mirror

Flash tube

Synthetic ruby crystal

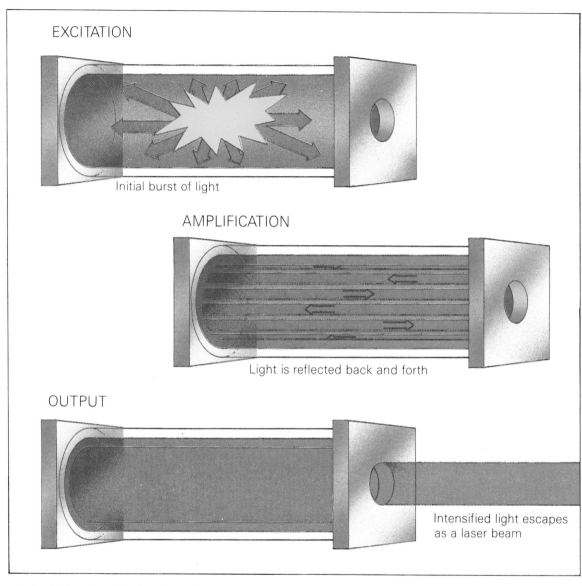

EXCITATION

Initial burst of light

AMPLIFICATION

Light is reflected back and forth

OUTPUT

Intensified light escapes
as a laser beam

This diagram shows how laser light is produced.

all the light that hits it. The other is only partially reflective. As the light bounces back and forth it builds up in intensity until it is strong enough to burst through the partially reflecting mirror. Lasing is then said to occur.

Types of laser

Lasers can be made not only from solids, such as ruby crystal, but also from many different liquids and gases. A recent development is the use of semiconductor materials, such as those found in microchips, as the active medium. The source of energy, too, can vary. Usually, this is an electric current or the light from a nearby flash tube or another laser. However, in some lasers, the system is powered by the heat produced by a chemical reaction. When mixed together, certain chemicals react violently to produce heat, which in turn excites the atoms of the chemicals into lasing.

The colour of the beam depends on the substance the laser is made from. A helium-neon (HeNe) gas laser and a ruby crystal laser produce a red beam, a krypton (Kr)

Lasers can sometimes be used to excite other lasers into producing a laser beam.

laser produces a blue-green or orange beam, while a 'dye' laser can produce any one of several colours. Some gas lasers can produce beams of infra-red or ultraviolet light, both of which are invisible to the human eye.

A laser's power is measured in watts, like an electric light bulb. A low-powered laser may be rated at only 5 watts, while a high-powered type may be measured at several million watts. However, lasers can produce a beam as a series of extremely short bursts, or pulses, of light or as a single steady beam. They are said to be either a pulsed

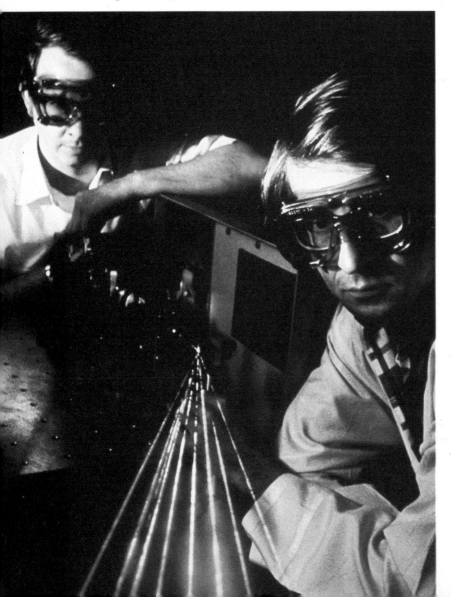

Dye lasers can produce beams of any one of several colours.

A fingerprint, which would normally be invisible to the naked eye, glows brightly under laser light.

or a continuous wave laser. Pulsed lasers are the most powerful as their light energy is concentrated into rapid pulses, each of which may last less than one billionth of a second.

Lasers in industry

Lasers are used in industry to cut, drill, weld or engrave such materials as steel, glass, plastic and ceramic. Continuous carbon dioxide (CO_2) gas lasers are often used to cut and weld, and their high power is due not so much to the amount of energy they produce, but to the amount of energy that is focused on a target. For example, sunlight appears to have little energy. But if you focus the rays of the sun on to a sheet of paper using a magnifying glass, the small, concentrated spot of sunlight will burn a hole in the paper. Similarly, a laser beam can be focused by a lens or mirror to a spot the size of the full stop at the end of this sentence. The concentration of energy can be so

Some lasers can cut through diamond – the hardest material known to man.

great that the beam will instantly boil away metals and even diamond, the hardest of all materials.

Cutting and drilling

As cutting and drilling tools, lasers have the advantages of being fast acting, not wearing out, and they can be used with great accuracy and precision. Because a laser beam puts little or no pressure on the surface of a material, it can cut through it cleanly. The beam produces narrow cut lines, without ripping or burning the material. When drilling, a laser beam does not produce any tiny fragments of waste material, or swarf, that will clog up a conventional mechanical drill.

An ordinary mechanical drill leaves swarf around the hole drilled in a metal block; a laser leaves a clean hole with no swarf.

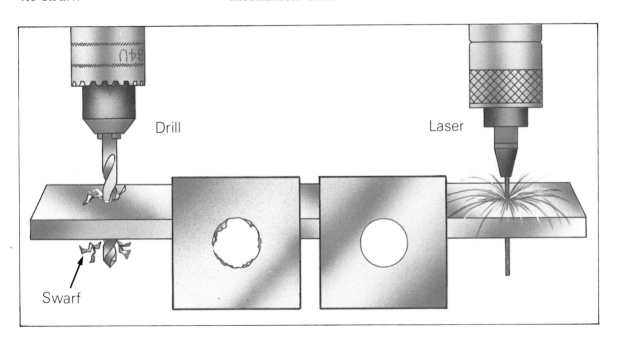

Drill

Laser

Swarf

In the car industry, lasers are used to cut and drill the moving metal parts. In the plastics and glass industries, they are used for cutting up large sheets of perspex or window glass, or for punching holes in a material to make sieves such as those used in cookery or chemistry. Laser beams are also used to cut out shapes in cloth, often burning their way through several layers of the fabric at a time. The beam neatly seals the cut edges, preventing them from fraying.

13

Engraving and welding

The precision and easy control of a laser beam makes it an excellent tool for engraving and welding. In engraving, the beam is made sufficiently powerful to boil away, or

This man is demonstrating how a laser can be used to drill a hole in metal block.

vaporize, only the top few millimetres of the material, be it in metal, glass or ceramic. When a laser is being used to weld, say, two sheets of steel together, the beam melts, but does not vaporize, the metal. As the beam moves away, the molten metal quickly solidifies, forming a strong, smooth weld. The metal either side of the weld is not weakened as it would be if an oxy-acetylene torch was used.

Lasers are now used to cut the most intricate of shapes and to work in areas inaccessible to ordinary tools. The laser itself can be kept stationary and the beam directed to where it is wanted via an optical fibre, or by reflecting the beam through a series of mirrors. Much of this work is computer controlled. Instructions about the speed, depth and power of the beam are fed into the computer. The computer then controls the strength of the laser, and directs and focuses the beam on to the target. In the nuclear power industry, computer-controlled and computer-guided lasers are used to work on spent uranium fuel rods that, being radioactive, cannot be handled directly.

Surface treatments

High-powered lasers are also used in industry to modify the properties of metals. For instance, by heating the surface of steel with a laser and then rapidly cooling it, the metal is hardened. Car parts subjected to great wear and tear, such as gear wheels, are treated in this way.

Lasers can be used to join two sheets of metal together. As the laser moves across the surfaces to be joined, the metal melts and then solidifies forming a strong weld.

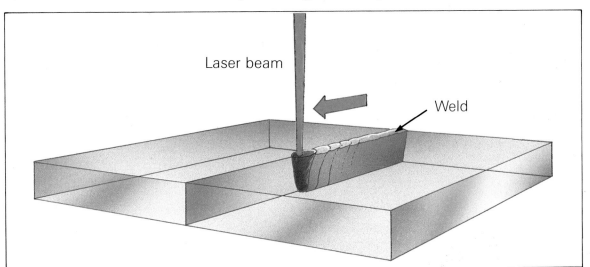

Laser beam

Weld

Left A high-powered laser drilling holes in a block of metal. Lasers have the advantage of not wearing out as no part of the equipment comes into contact with the material being cut or drilled.

Scientists are now experimenting with lasers as tools for plating metals. The surface of a cheap metal is heated so that other metals such as silver, chromium or copper can be deposited on the surface in much greater quantities than was possible using conventional electroplating techniques. Some chromium-plated tools and car parts, and silver-plated cutlery, for instance, are produced using lasers.

What next?

Lasers will take on new roles, as the demands of industry change. It is perhaps in the electronics and energy industries that lasers will have the most impact. Already, lasers are being used to make very fine welds, or microwelds, to solder connections on printed circuit boards and to weld silicon chips into their cases. Currently under development

Right A high-powered laser in action, cutting shapes in a sheet of plastic.

is the use of a laser to simplify the manufacture of microchips. Normally, a complicated sequence of processing steps involving light-sensitive materials, masks and etching is needed to make the electronic circuits on a microchip. The new technique will involve coating parts of the microchip crystal with a special material and then directing a laser beam on to selected parts of it to produce the circuits.

Being developed now is the use of laser light in optical transistors and microchips, called transphasors. Within a transphasor, laser light is changed into ordinary light. The

Using an arrangement of mirrors, lasers beams can be directed simply and easily.

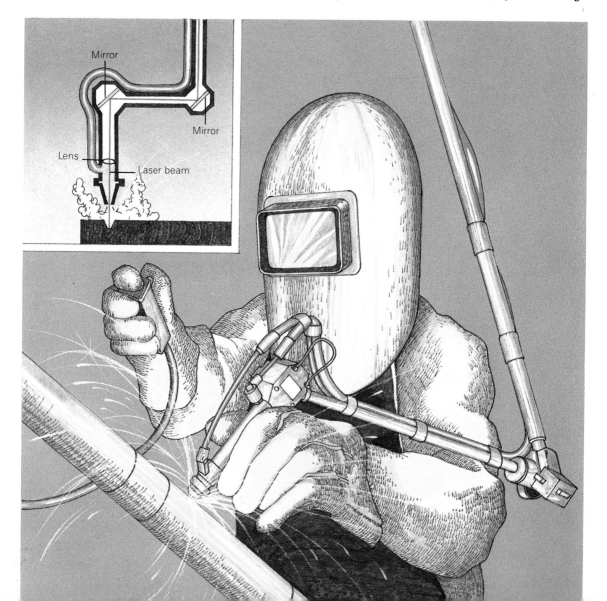

Part of the Shiva laser reactor currently under development in America.

action of changing from one type of light to the other is like a switch. Transphasors could be used in a computer as switches that control the flow of data around the machine. Working with light rather than electric currents, transphasors can operate many times faster than ordinary microchips.

One of the most exciting prospects for high-powered lasers is in providing man with a virtually unlimited source of energy. Scientists are investigating the use of lasers to produce controlled thermonuclear explosions that will generate electrical energy.

When the nuclei of two hydrogen atoms join, or fuse, together, they form a helium atom, giving off a vast amount of heat and light energy in the process. In the sun, this process is going on all the time. Nuclear fusion requires incredibly high temperatures. Only lasers can produce such heat. Currently under development in America is a giant laser reactor, called Shiva, that is capable of generating 25 million, million watts of power. In theory, laser fusion is possible with this vast energy source.

19

Lasers in medicine

The ability of lasers to deliver a precise amount of energy with pinpoint accuracy, and to cut and weld materials in inaccessible areas, has made them of great use in medicine.

Lasers are now commonly used for the treatment of some eye disorders, skin diseases and for surgery on some internal organs. They are also used in dentistry, to burn away damaged tooth material.

Injury or disease of the eye can cause small blood vessels at the back of the eye to burst. A laser beam can be directed through the front of the eye and focused on the bleeding vessels to burn them away. Some eye defects occur when the retina, the light-sensitive part of the eye, becomes

This surgeon is using a laser to weld the patient's retina back into place.

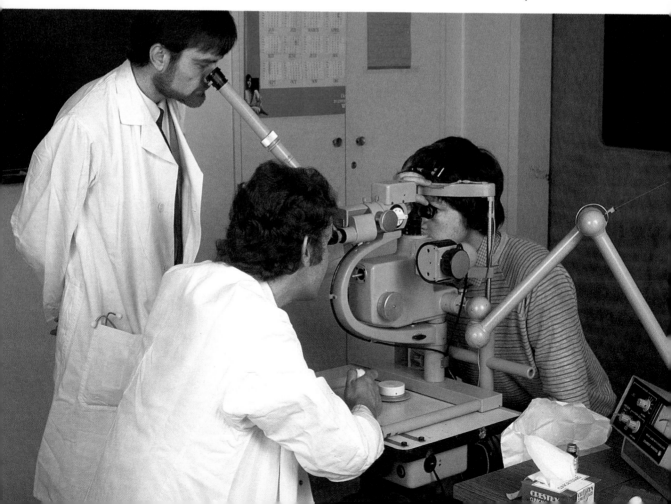

Right and below *Lasers are used to remove skin markings such as the red birth marks known as 'port wine stains'.*

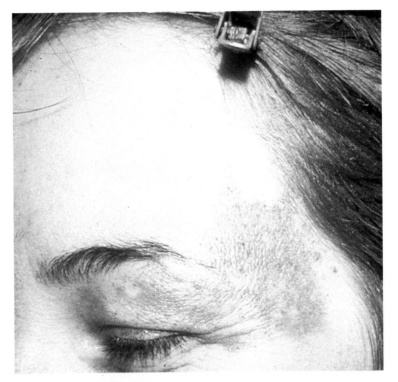

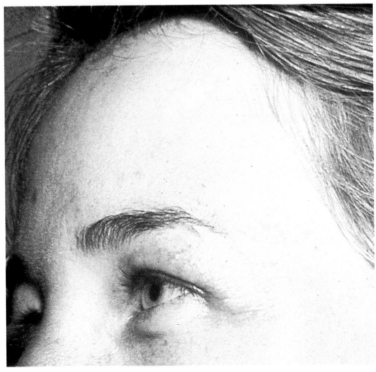

detached from the back of the eyeball. Laser light welds the retina back into place. Both types of operation are painless, and take only a few minutes.

Doctors now use lasers to remove birthmarks, tattoos and warts on the skin. The laser beam burns away the paper-thin layers of marked skin tissue so that new, un-coloured tissue can grow to replace it. Cosmetic surgeons use lasers to remove wrinkles in skin and to perform face-lift operations.

In medical operations, lasers are to some extent replacing the surgeon's scalpel. The intense heat of the laser beam seals up small blood vessels around the cut, and so prevents excessive bleeding. Using an endoscope, a flexible tube about as thick as a finger containing optical fibres and thin tubes, a surgeon can remove tumours, cancerous growths, ulcers and gall stones without opening up the patient. The surgeon passes the endoscope down the patient's throat to the area needing treatment, and directs the laser on to the target using the optical fibres. The thin tubes provide water and air to clean the area being worked on by the laser beam.

In America, lasers have been used to clear blocked blood vessels. A catheter, a very fine tube, is passed into the patient's artery. Inside the catheter are optical fibres that deliver the beam on to the fibrous tissue causing the blockage.

Future uses of lasers may well be in the fields of genetic engineering and pain relief. Japanese researchers have used a laser to help transfer DNA, the genetic material of cells, from one cell to another. Directed on to target cells, the laser beam opens up tiny holes in the cells' outer membrane for just enough time to allow the new DNA to enter. The technique could be used to help scientists identify cancer-causing genes, develop disease-resistant and higher-yielding crops, and to mass-produce proteins for animal feedstocks.

It has been discovered that low-powered laser light, when directed on to nerve centres, alleviates pain. This may herald the use of lasers in acupuncture – the newest of technologies being used for one of the oldest of cures.

The surgeon in this picture is using a laser beam to perform a delicate operation with the help of an endoscope. The inset shows the laser beam which travels along optical fibres inside the endoscope.

22

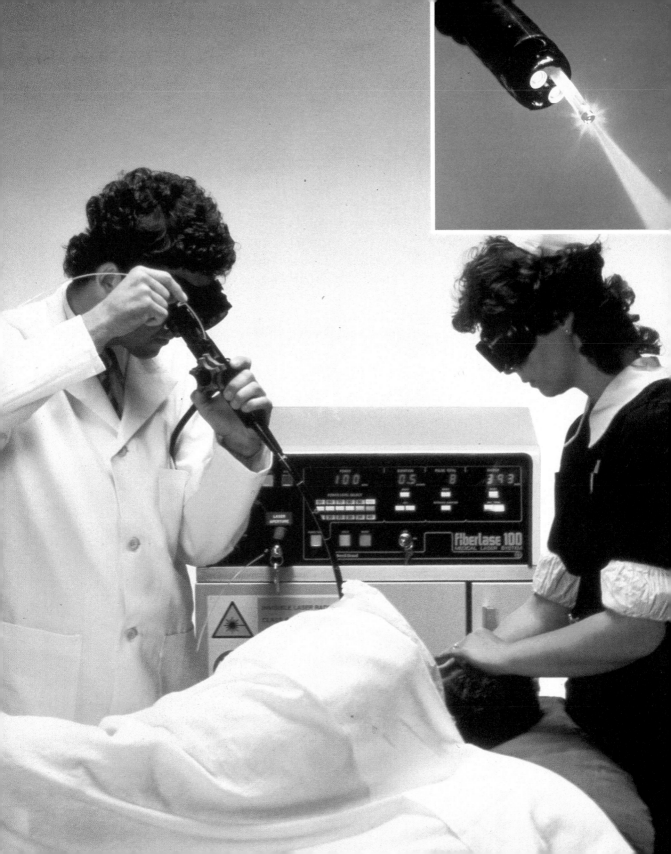

Measuring and aligning with lasers

Light travels at a speed of 300 million metres a second. By timing how long it takes for a pulse of laser light to travel from one point to another, large distances can be measured with great accuracy. Surveyors mapping an area commonly use such laser 'tape measures'. On a grander scale, the distance between the earth and moon can be measured by lasers. A pulse of laser light is projected at the moon where a mirror, left by astronauts, reflects the light back to the earth. The timing of the pulse's round-trip gives a distance that is accurate to within 5 centimetres (2 inches).

Surveyors use lasers for measuring distances.

24

The laser beam in this picture was used to measure the distance to the moon. It was aimed at a mirror left by Apollo 11 astronauts on the moon's surface (inset).

The height of clouds can be measured in the same way. Water droplets in the clouds act as tiny reflectors directing the pulses of laser light back to a receiver on the ground. The receiver automatically works out the exact distance. Such measurements are of use in meteorology, pollution control and air traffic safety.

In 1976, NASA launched LAGEOS, a satellite covered with tiny mirrors that reflect laser beams. The satellite is used to study tiny movements in the earth's crust. Beams are directed towards LAGEOS from ground stations along major faults in the crust, such as the San Andreas fault in California, in order to pinpoint the relative positions of the stations. By constantly monitoring these positions, any movements of the crust are detected immediately.

Interferometry

Minute measurements can be made with lasers using an instrument called an interferometer. This splits a laser beam in two, reflects each half on to separate mirrors, one fixed near to the device and the other being moveable and set some distance away, and then recombines them into a single bright beam. When the mirror is moved, the two

The LAGEOS satellite is used to measure movements in the earth's crust. The inset shows the LAGEOS satellite being tested before its launch into space.

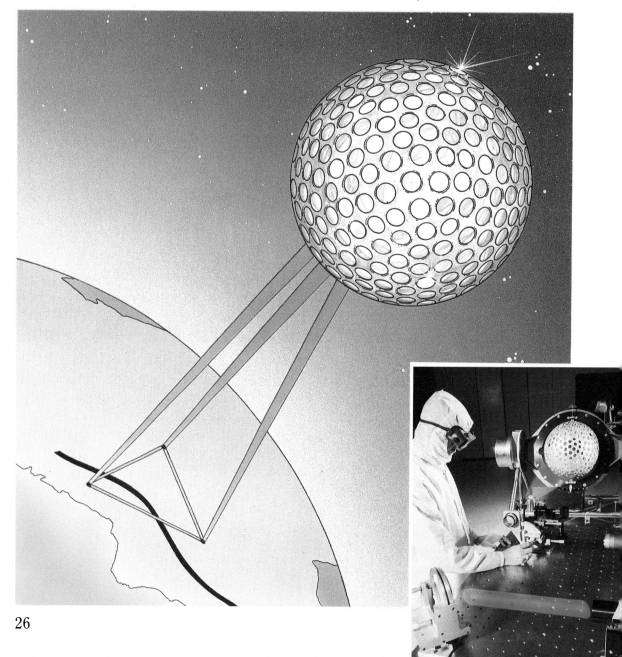

Laser light is used to test the way rapidly moving objects behave at high speeds. Here a jet's turbine is being tested in a wind tunnel.

laser beams do not recombine but, instead, 'interfere' with one another, creating a fuzzy, ripple-like pattern known as interference fringes. A detector in the interferometer counts the interference fringes to work out the precise distance the mirror moved.

Laser interferometers are used to measure tiny movements in the earth's crust caused by earthquakes or underground nuclear explosions. The laser, the beam-splitter and the fixed mirror are mounted on one granite pillar sunk into bedrock, while the other mirror is mounted on a second pillar some distance away. A tremor causes the mirrors to move in different ways relative to one another, producing interference fringes. Minute movements of the crust can then be detected.

Alignment

As a laser beam is rod-like and spreads out very little, even over large distances, it can be used as a kind of plumb line or spirit level to check that things are exactly vertical or horizontal. It can also be used to check that objects align perfectly. Alignment lasers are used for accuracy in the laying of oil pipelines and sewer pipes, in the construction of motorways, tunnels, bridges and skyscrapers, and in the surveying of large tracks of land. The structure of super-tankers and large cargo ships is monitored by alignment lasers for movements caused by heavy seas, or by the filling and emptying of the tanks and holds.

This device uses a laser beam to measure the height and thickness of smoke plumes from factory chimneys as part of a programme of air pollution research.

Chemical measurements

Every chemical absorbs light in a unique way. Lasers can identify the different chemicals in a substance by analysing the quantity and wavelengths of the light it absorbs. Analysis by light is known as spectroscopy.

Laser spectroscopy is used to monitor the pollution of the air and water, and so keep a check on the discharge of chemicals from factories and the levels of car exhaust fumes in the air of cities.

Experimentation with and the application of lasers in measurement and alignment work has led to a variety of possible new uses for lasers. For example, in America scientists are now developing laser canes that will help blind people to get around. The canes emit pulses of infra-red laser light that are reflected back for analysis by detectors in the canes, and sounds are emitted that vary according to the distances and types of objects that are ahead. Some fire prevention systems now use laser spectroscopy to monitor levels of inflammable vapours: when the levels are too high, alarms are set off automatically. In the chemical industry, laser beams are used to initiate and check the rate of chemical reactions, and to break up some chemical compounds in order to purify substances. There are plans to use lasers to study the structure of atoms, the building bricks of all matter.

Lasers at war

The first large-scale use of lasers was for military purposes. During the Vietnam War of the 1960s, America developed and utilized laser rangefinders and tracking and guidance systems. A typical laser rangefinder consists of a sighting telescope for aiming the light beam, a transmitter and receiver, and a computer. The rangefinder is aimed at the target and switched on. A pulse of high-intensity infra-red laser light is transmitted and at the same instant an electric

A laser designator for use by ground troops.

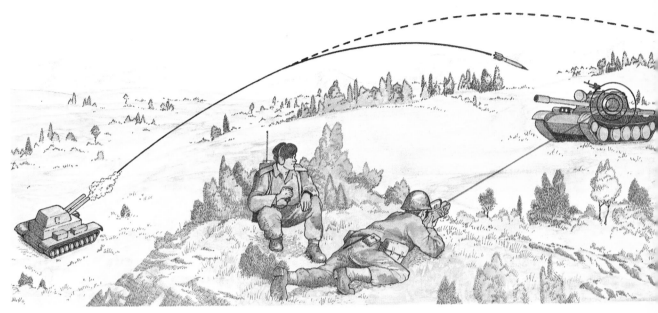

Missiles or shells can be guided to a target using a laser designator. The dotted line shows the missile's normal flight path.

timer starts. Light returning from the target stops the timer. The computer, by measuring the length of time the pulse took to travel to the target and back, calculates the range. The result is fed straight to the weapon's automatic fire control system.

More recent developments in laser rangefinding devices are hand-held binoculars and rifle sights. They each contain a small, battery-powered laser crystal. The range is displayed on a screen within the instrument that is viewed through the eyepiece.

Laser tracking and guidance systems are used to home in gun shells and missiles on to a target that is being marked by laser light from a 'designator' carried by ground troops or an aircraft. The designator contains a laser that transmits pulses of infra-red light. Once the target is located, the missile – or shell – is fired towards it. A 'seeker' device in the nose of the missile picks up, or senses, the laser light reflected from the target and guides the weapon down to make a direct hit.

Both laser rangefinders and tracking and guidance instruments operate more quickly and effectively than similar conventional devices, and they can be used day or

night. However, there are now available laser-warning receivers that will alert the crew of, say, a tank when their vehicle is being illuminated by infra-red light from a laser rangefinder or designator. Precise details of how the receiver works are secret, but it is likely that it works by detecting and identifying certain wavelengths of light. With this knowledge, troops under attack could transmit laser light of a similar wavelength to try and block the electronic sensors trying to locate them.

Tanks and armoured cars can be fitted with laser rangefinders for pinpointing targets on the battlefield.

Ray guns

In 1983, in America, a continuous-beam carbon dioxide (CO_2) gas laser housed in a converted Boeing 707 jet was used to shoot down air-to-air missiles. The Russians are believed to have devised surveillance satellites equipped with lasers that can destroy enemy satellites and missiles when first spotted. And from West Germany recently came plans for a network of about 250 laser-carrying satellites, orbiting 550 kilometres (340 miles) above the earth, which could destroy several hundred missiles on their way into space.

As laser beams can travel through space easily, they make ideal weapons to knock out planes, missiles and satellites. However, such lasers will need to be extremely large and powerful, and so the lasers, and the satellites

This converted airliner houses a laser for shooting down air-to-air missiles.

which carry them, will be difficult and expensive to construct, and slow to manoeuvre once operational in space. Yet America has committed some $200 million in 1984 alone to developing the 'Space Laser Triad', a group of three orbiting laser battle stations, and a laser tracking system to search and destroy Soviet nuclear missiles. The death-ray space cannons of the film *Star Wars* may soon become a reality!

Satellites equipped with lasers could be used to destroy incoming nuclear missiles in space.

Holography

Holography is a form of three-dimensional photography. It involves the illumination of an object with laser light and the recording of all the light waves reflected on a flat, light-sensitive glass plate or film. The image appears to have the same size, height, breadth and depth as the original object. When looking at a hologram, the image can be observed from all sides. With an ordinary photograph, the image looks the same no matter where you view it from.

Holograms are made using special arrangements of laser beams and light-sensitive glass plates or film. This diagram shows one such arrangement for making a hologram.

In industry, the main uses of holography are to detect stresses and strains and to measure small movements or vibrations in objects. This involves interferometry (see page

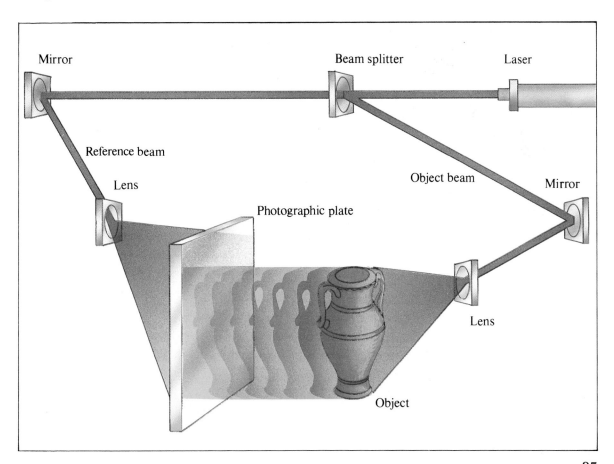

Mirror

Beam splitter

Laser

Reference beam

Lens

Object beam

Mirror

Photographic plate

Lens

Object

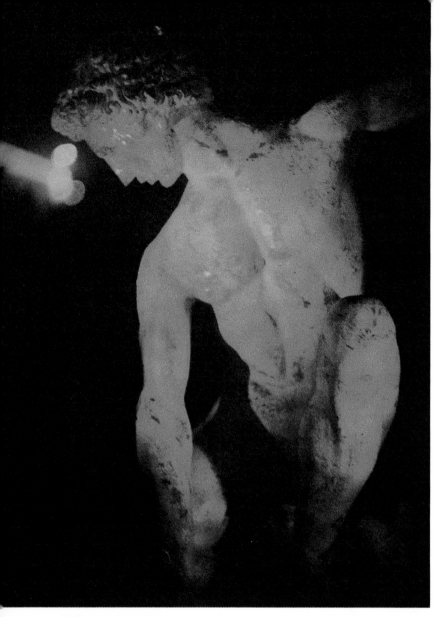

26). With holographic interferometry, a comparison is drawn between a hologram of an object made in normal conditions and one made under experimental conditions. Any changes in the shape of the object appear as changes in the interference pattern. The technique is used to study defects in, for example, car tyres, rifle bores, musical instruments and jet turbine blades.

More recently, lasers producing very short pulses of light have been used to produce holograms that can freeze high-speed motion. The holograms can record details of the movement of streams of particles in fluids. They have become important aids in the study of the airflow over car bodies and aircraft wings, and the movement of water through pipes and tubes.

In the art world, holographic interferometry is used to monitor the effects of temperature and humidity changes on oil paintings, and to detect where paint is coming away from the backing canvas or wood.

Holograms can be printed on to any material coated with a light-sensitive emulsion. Credit cards bearing a strip of a forgery-proof holographic pattern are being developed for use in computerized cashpoint machines and pay telephones. Holograms printed on silvery plastic are used for book and record covers and for decorative papers and wrappers. Jewellery and badges bearing holograms are popular.

Some holograms can be viewed by shining a laser beam on the holographic plate. Others can be lit by ordinary white light from a normal light source.

Information storage

A typical crystal has many sides or faces. A hologram can be stored on each one. By repeatedly turning a crystal through a very small angle and recording a holographic image on each face, up to 1,000 pieces of information can

be stored on the crystal. This technique is being developed to store records of works of art and computer data. The advantages of this technique are, firstly, the information takes up less space than it does in existing photographic archives and computer memories. Secondly, only a small part of a hologram is needed to reconstruct the image. Even if the crystal is damaged, it is probable that some part of it will remain intact to retrieve the information, so it is a very safe method of storing information.

Holograms are also being used to store confidential information such as personal, medical and financial records. The information is stored partly on one hologram, partly on another, so that both are needed to retrieve all the information. With the need for more data security, this application of holograms is likely to become more commonplace.

The patterns of lines that you can see in this picture are interference fringes. Holographic interferometry is used to study defects in such things as rifle bores, car tyres and jet turbine blades.

38

Communicating with lasers

An increasingly important use for lasers is in the storing, processing and transmission of information. Lasers can do these things more quickly, cheaply, accurately and efficiently than any other system of transmission.

Laser beams can carry messages through the air, but the beams are blocked by anything that gets in the way, and are badly affected by clouds and fog, so open-air laser communication is limited. However, the laser signals are almost impossible to intercept so they have an important military use over short distances. Soldiers equipped with

Optical fibres are hair-thin strands of glass. They are so fine that dozens of them will pass through the eye of a needle at the same time.

This telephone engineer is using special equipment to join optical fibre cables together.

portable laser receiver/transmitters can relay messages to one another, conditions permitting, safe in the knowledge that the enemy cannot eavesdrop on their conversation. In space, where there are no obstacles and no weather, lasers are important for the sending of signals to and from military satellites.

Fibre-optic links

Optical fibres are hair-thin glass threads that can transmit light over long distances with very little loss of intensity. Rays of laser or ordinary light travelling along an optical fibre are reflected off the sides so that none escape. The fibres can carry much more information than radio waves and are considerably cheaper to make than the copper cables that currently carry most telephone and telex signals. Optical fibre links cannot be bugged or tapped.

In an optical fibre telephone network, speech is converted into electrical signals, which stimulate a laser to fire tiny pulses of laser light. The pulses are directed into the optical fibre, which conducts the light signal to its destination. Devices called repeaters are placed along the optical fibre every few kilometres. These boost the signal to allow the light pulses to travel great distances. At the other end of the telephone line, the laser light is converted back into electrical signals and then back into speech in the telephone earpiece.

Laser-optical fibre links are now being used to carry many telephone messages and computer data, and they have also made possible cable television, video telephones, and facsimile units – machines that can transmit and receive copies of documents and printed pictures via a telephone line.

Optical discs

Lasers are used to 'write' and 'read' information, as well as to send messages. The information is usually stored in binary form, the on/off code used by computers. Video discs, audio discs, bar codes and some identity cards use this technology.

Video discs store sound and TV pictures. They resemble

plastic long-playing records, but they have a metallic surface covered by a protective coating of clear plastic. Electrical signals recorded with a video camera or microphone are fed into a microchip. This controls a tiny laser beam that is projected on to the disc, etching a pattern of tiny pits in the disc's surface. To read the information, a laser beam in a video disc player is reflected from the pits into an electronic device that changes the light signals into

Video discs are made in clean, dust-free rooms.

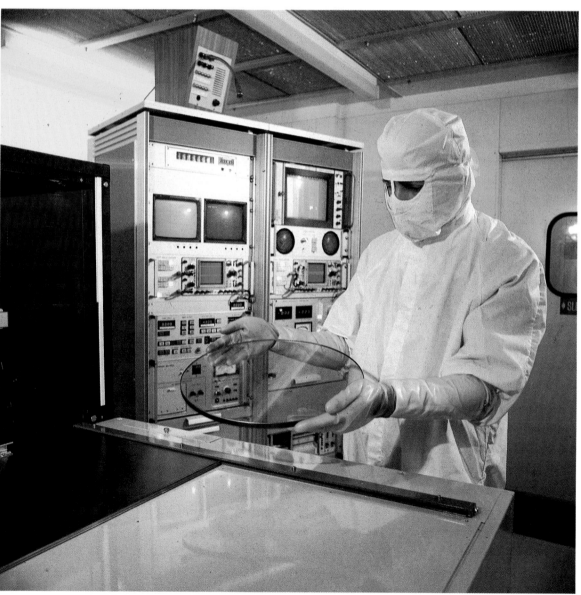

A video disc system showing a video disc, a video disc player and a TV to show the pictures.

electrical signals. The player then converts the electrical signals into pictures and sound. Each disc can store an hour of video, or 54,000 still pictures.

Audio discs, which are like video discs, store only sound. They are also known as compact or digital discs. The quality of sound reproduced by these discs is far better than long-playing records or magnetic tapes.

In the future, computer data and programs will be stored on optical discs. Although conventional magnetic tapes and discs are excellent ways for storing computer information, the recording often deteriorates when they are played many times. Optical discs have proved to be more hard-wearing, and they can store vast amounts of information, making them ideal as permanent recorders of information.

Bar code readers

Lasers are commonly used in supermarkets and libraries to read the bar codes stamped on the packaging of goods and on book covers and record sleeves. The code is of a series of lines of varying thickness, which represent an item number and price, or a book or record classification number. At the check-out point, a laser wand is used to read the code, reflecting a beam off the pattern of lines back to a light detector. The information is then fed to a central computer for later reference.

A laser bar code reader production line.

A supermarket check-out counter with a laser bar code reader in use.

Laser printing

Most books, magazines and newspapers are printed off metal plates on which the words and pictures are engraved on the surface. Lasers can be used to engrave the plates. Controlled by electrical signals, a laser beam cuts tiny grooves for the words and pictures in the metal plates.

With the ability to send, receive, read, write and store information, laser communications systems are unequalled in all respects. Their application in the new field of information technology has made the electronic office and working and shopping from home a reality. Almost certainly it is in the area of communications that lasers will become, more and more, a part of everyday life.

Glossary

Atom One of the tiny particles of which all matter is made up.

Amplify To increase in strength.

Carbon dioxide A colourless, odourless gas which is present in the atmosphere.

Frequency The number of peaks in a wave of light that pass a point in one second.

Hologram A three-dimentional recording of an image on a flat photographic film or plate using laser light as the means of illumination.

Interference pattern The pattern of light and dark lines formed when two or more beams of light pass through one another.

Interferometer An instrument designed to produce interference patterns. It is used to measure the wavelength of light or to measure very small distances accurately.

Laser A device which emits a beam of coherent light which behaves as if it were a single continuous wave. The term comes from the first letter of each word in the phrase that describes how it works – Light Amplification by Stimulated Emission of Radiation.

Light In the past this word was used to describe electromagnetic radiation that is visible to the eye. Now it includes wave-lengths that cannot be seen such as ultra-violet and infra-red light.

Optical fibres Very thin strands of glass through which pulses of light can be sent.

Prism A wedge-shaped block of glass or quartz which splits up white light into different colours.

Spectrum The whole range of wavelengths and frequencies of light, from radio waves to beyond X-rays. It is often used to describe the seven colours that make up visible light – red, orange, yellow, green, blue, indigo and violet.

Wavelength The distance between successive peaks of a light wave.

Further reading

If you would like to find out more about lasers, you may like to read the following books:

Lasers by William Burroughs (Wayland, 1982)
Lasers by Lynn Myring and Maurice Kimmitt (Usborne, 1984)
Lasers by Robin McKie (Franklin Watts, 1983)

Lasers by William Burroughs (Collins, 1984)

You may find that a nearby museum has a permanent exhibition of lasers and holograms. Many art galleries also display holograms, and there may be a shop in your town which sells small holograms and holographic jewellery.

Index

Acknowledgements

The publisher would like to thank all those who provided pictures on the following pages: Barr & Stroud Limited 23 (both); British Telecommunications PLC 40; Bill Donohoe 18, 24, 26, 29, 31, 34; Ferranti 17; PHOTRI cover, 2–3, 10, 12, 14, 19, 25 (both), 26 (inset), 27, 30, 32, 33, 37, 38; St. Bartholomew's Hospital 20; Science Photo Library 4 (T. Malyon), 16 (R. Ellis), 36 (J. Mason), 39 (J. Walsh), 45 (P. Shambroom); Spectra-Physics 9, 11, 21 (both), 44; THORN EMI 42, 43; Malcolm S. Walker 5, 6, 7, 8, 13, 15, 35.